D1785626

PYROTECHNICS

HILDA MUNDY

PYROTECHNICS
A SPINELESS ESSAY OF ULTRAIST LITERATURE

HILDA MUNDY

WE HEARD YOU LIKE BOOKS
LOS ANGELES, CALIFORNIA

PUBLISHED BY WE HEARD YOU LIKE BOOKS
A Division of U2603 LLC
5419 Hollywood Blvd, Ste C-231 Los Angeles CA 90027

http://weheardyoulikebooks.com/

Joshua Mast
Publisher

Brandon Creighton
Co-Publisher

Distributed by SCB Distributors

ISBN: 978-0996421867
Copyright © Hilda Mundy, Jessica Sequira

All Rights Reserved

Typesetting & Cover by M Kitchell

October 2017

First Edition

10 9 8 7 6 5 4 3 2 1

TABLE OF CONTENTS

TRANSLATOR'S NOTE

JESSICA SEQUERIA

My edition of *Pirotecnia* has a red cover and a title spelled out in bold black cursive. It was printed by Chile-based Libros de la Mujer Rota, an independent publisher run by writer Claudia Aplabaza and named after Simone de Beauvoir's *The Woman Destroyed*, and the bold design is a good indication of the contents awaiting the reader inside. The tone of the poems is intense, ludic, aggravated, sarcastic and non-romantic at the same time. Their attention to detail, no matter the ennui the author may profess, seems to reflect a deep attention to and love for life.

I tried not to deviate too far from the original words, as much as is possible with a translation of poetry, an enterprise something like climbing a melting glacier. Yet it was impossible in some places to prevent an "estranging" effect in English. Partly this has to do with the author herself; even where I could find a reasonable equivalent, the original often read "strangely" in Spanish. Hilda exercised a great freedom in making up words, chaining concepts and following lateral trains of thought; hers is a modernist prose. Talking about inventions such as the telephone and tram, she brings her prose up to date as well.

Even when Hilda writes about everyday things, such as the lottery or red nail polish, these quickly start to seem bizarre, almost grotesque, in the same way as a familiar word when you repeat it many times, or furniture when you change its position in the room. Disorientation moored by irony is what follows, but the dissonance is strangely pleasant. Contemporary readers may be more accustomed to this "avant-garde" tone than readers of Hilda's day; in English it evokes poets like Pound and the Vorticists of the magazine *Blast!*, and in Spanish it points to the Ultraist movement originating in Spain, picked up in Latin America by Borges among others.

Marked by its use of metaphor and startling images, creative uses of typography, neologisms and rejection of rhyme, the Ultraist movement was clearly the tradition in which Mundy was working. She subtitled her book *Ensayo miedoso de literatura ultraísta*, which I have chosen to translate as "A spineless essay of Ultraist literature", rendering "miedoso" as "spineless" rather than "fearful", "cowardly" or "faint-hearted", to reflects what I see as its spiritedness. This is ironic, and there is much in Hilda's work that is not to be taken at face value, down to her name itself. Hilda Mundy is a pseudonym, the name of an English actress of the period; Mundy's real name was Laura Villanueva Rocabado.

Mundy channeled her irony and self-conscious free verse innovations into irreverent tirades full of both sly humor and lyricism. Content-wise, almost nothing seems out of bound for her. Technology, domestic life, sexual mores, body shape and walks around the city are all discussed, in an antihistorical, antiauthoritarian, mythologizing vein.

Claiming to despise boredom, Mundy defends an unpredictable existence made up of constant new sensations. This is why her Dadaist gesture of publishing just one book during her lifetime is perhaps an aesthetic choice, rather than a necessity that can be explained away by marriage to fellow poet Antonio Ávila Jiménez. Hilda's work appears to have consumed itself in its own intensity, giving way to life. Or is this too rhetoric? For this really was not the last thing Hilda wrote; a collection of pieces, *Cosas de Fondo: Impressiones de la Guerra del Chaco y otros escritos* [Vital Things: Impressions of the Chaco War and Other Writings] was published posthumously.

What does seem clear is that the sensations she alludes to in her poem are not primarily physical, but perceptual. The new experiences she seeks are primarily those of the spirit. "When ennui threatens me, to the point / I put myself in very strange roles, / I imagine myself as: [...]" she writes, before listing an eclectic array of professions she would never perform in reality. It is enough to imagine living a different life; one need not actually live it. This freedom to imagine is perhaps the only thing Mundy will never attack.

There is one concept I wish I could translate better, which is linked to the title, "pirotecnia". Hilda's pyrotechnics, her "sparklers", are a play on the phrase "fuego fatuo". To represent nothing is a "fatuo" property of pyrotechnics, Hilda notes on the first page; "fatuo" on its own simply means "inane" or "foolish". This is in part a knowing, self-deprecating comment by Hilda about her own work.

As an idiomatic expression, however, "fuego fatuo" is one of the most beautiful phrases in the Spanish language. It can mean "will-'o-the-wisp", "spook lights", "jack-'o-lantern", "fleeting fancy", all those lovely things that are whimsical and fleeting. Mundy adores the coquetting sentence, the suggestion, the ability to change one's mind, the allusion. What is *not* said is as important as what is, and she refers multiple times to the virtues of ellipses, which allow the imagination to be carried away. This is an interpretive freedom available to the reader as well. For this reason, to be true to Hilda's vision, I think it best to keep this note brief. May the reader discover for herself in all their glory Hilda's bright exploding Roman candles of the imagination.

PROLOGUE
HILDA MUNDA, THE AVANT-GARDE

EDMUNDO PAZ SOLDAN

When we talk about literary avant-gardes we tend to imagine a group of writers planning manifestos, participating in *happenings*, and editing books together. In many Latin American countries not everything was so collective; that was the case with Bolivia, where Hilda Mundy (1912-1982) was the only avant-garde writer (and one of the few female avant-garde writers on the continent). In the '30s, when Mundy wrote, Bolivian poetry was still attached to forms of modernism from which the rest of the continent had moved on; it would have to wait until the end of the '50s and start of the '70s for renewal to occur. This may explain why the merits of the Oruro poet's small body of work are only now being appreciated.

Hilda Mundy, the pseudonym of Laura Villanueva Rocabado, published just one book in her lifetime: *Pirotecnia,* subtitled "A spineless essay of Ultraist literature" (1936). The book was forgotten until 2004, when the Bolivian publishing house Ediciones La Mariposa Mundial printed a new edition of this highly valuable work. Mundy's seventy prose texts attempt to capture the noise of the metropolis in the new century, the product of technological transformations and changes in sensibility and behavior. Her work comments on the

11

fledgling modernity in the west of the country, including the possibility of alternatives to marriage and the new roles aspired to by women ("...she now feels herself a suffragist... chauffeur... aviator... engine driver... concert performer... boxer..."). Paradoxically, Mundy didn't support the proto-feminist movements of her age.

The author sings her praises to electricity ("The hulking street light developed into an electric light bulb through a miracle of the Empress of Light...") and plays with the changes in perspective during a journey in a tram: "On the platform with all the last minute passengers, two worlds appeared to me: travelers in the tram seated childlike facing one another, and the evasive artistic panorama of the city [...] Science and art for the modest sum of twenty centavos!". Her writing registers technological advances — the telephone, the public streetlight — and new urban settings — the theater, the sweet shop, the stadium — and admires them, while also showing doubt about the toll of progress. She writes of the automobile, for instance, that "those traveling in it accustomed to the landscape disappearing behind them, also long for the disappearance of humanity". She accepts the modern cult of velocity, but prefers the calm movement of the tram to the frenzy of automobiles.

Literature may be predestined to failure, but one can discover "joy" in this. Mundy reveals herself to be a ludic spirit whose influences include Ramón Gómez de la Serna ("football is a Biblical sport"), the modernism of Julián del Casal, the futurism of Marinetti, Dadaism, and the typographical games so dear to the period. Her stylistic resources are various, but as a good Ultraist the central axis of her work is the daring metaphor: "a tempting neckline is the hall of a great hotel where the notes of a delightful jazz band can be heard, coming from the discrete and harmonic noise of necklaces of fantastic stones". Like Vicente Huidobro, Oquendo de Amat, Oliverio Girondo and other Latin American avant-gardes, she also chooses to work with the materiality of the text, at times using capital letters or italics and constantly recurring to ellipses. These latter ultimately become a metaphor for the type of light writing she praises in her short phrases, the opposite of the heavy rhetorical writing that must be transcended: "If you want to view life brightly, in a pantheistic and 'welcoming' light, nothing better than excessive use of ellipses [...] When you make lavish use of those little worlds in the typewriter, the article you're writing and your heart laugh at such cheek and irony."

At the age of only twenty-four and with such a promising work behind her, Hilda Mundy opted for silence. It would be logical to think she paid the price of many female writers of the period, who consumed by marriage and family (Mundy married two years after publishing *Pirotecnia*) didn't enjoy the possibility of continuing a literary career. Without opposing that reading, the poet and critic Eduardo Mitre proposes another, reminding us that in the epilogue of her book Mundy mentions three types of artists. One of them is the "Genius who remains silent... because to remain silent is to make thought flourish on the route to perfection". Mitre also points out that in her prologue Mundy suggests her texts are "fleeting fancies that represent nothing". Literature, in the Dadaist gesture of the author, is a useless project that must be questioned.

After her "pyrotechnics" and "attack on logic" that "does without authenticity and borders the absurd", the resulting gesture of the great artist is silence. In this, Mundy is as radical in her avant-garde ethos as Cesárea Tinajero in *The Savage Detectives*. Literature may be predestined to failure, but one can discover "joy" in this.

Edmundo Paz Soldán *was born in Cochabamba and is the author of* Río Fugitivo, El Delirio de Turing *and* Iris.

PYROTECHNICS

A SPINELESS ESSAY OF ULTRAIST LITERATURE

I offer this attack on logic.

It has no place or affiliation with the bibliographic field.

Because it lacks authenticity and borders the absurd.

Someone told me: Your book will be a laughable failure.

And I found joy in the prediction: imagining three-dozen readers laughing at the pages of my failure.

I don't want them to punish me with comments.

These brief treatises, scattered, rapid, "multicolor", represent: NOTHING. (Fleeting quality of pyrotechnics.)

We could say that this pamphlet is a line... — a comic strip, an aborted novel, that would have constituted a geometric drawing.

To clarify, I am useless for the latter.

I renounce my position and present myself to the public with 50 sparklers.

C'est fini.

PERSONAL WARNING TO THE READER

Press your finger in the inkpad
and cautiously go on

PART ONE

I

Overlapping, "discovered" and new
realities
are — more or less — pleasant...

If one is true to oneself as an eccentric,
there's no reason to cut the thread of that eccentricity, associating
with a logic common and vulgarized in the extreme.

The world of metaphors is so varied... so infinite
... that it lends itself to violation at any moment...

One can fantasize intensely... endlessly...
about: the man who passes, the woman who speaks, the idiot
who shyly sweeps the stones of the street...

How the unsuspected "cruxes" of things
are discovered!

With what micro-creator's pleasure one places quotes around
the desired word or "suspends" the tail end-intention
of a sentence with little black dots ...!

The bitter disagreement of the public floats in the emptiness.

An unusual "slowpokiness" compels one to unfurl
the eccentric index finger of language...

II

A theory:

Emotions are relative to people's weight.

A marvelously pale woman, with a heart condition
and 50 kilos of weight will better appreciate the splendor
of a sunset, the polyphony of a bird's chirping,
than an obese woman who can only appreciate the taste
of piglet...

It's no risk to say that a man with no appetite,
bilious, with a floating kidney, can feel the intrinsic
beauty of a work of art, more "supersensibly"
than another who is "porcinely" fat and satisfied...

The invertebrate emotions... subtle... ethereal...
emerged in a special way, like longed-for symptoms
during some afflictions...

Anemia... chlorosis... are lyrical illnesses...

Paleness, blueish under-eye circles reflect dreaming souls
... fragile... "dosed" with mystery...

Whereas — ruddiness, the rosy blush of a "camuesa"
apple, produce an impression of mediocrity,
vulgar acceptance of life, common concepts...

III

Impossible to imagine the creation of the world
except in a game of "football".

A game of "football" at a high level; origin-point
for the current vulgarized and decadent sport.

The handsome creator with his robust athletic complexion
(not skinny and weak like a cemetery overseer) would give
the first kick of the splendid game.

What magisterial stadium would host his training?

A quick-moving game of capers: In a direct
"shootout", he'd put the sun — a ball of fire — in the goal
of the sky. As an unknown defender slept, with
a push he'd make the moon — ball of light —
whirl fast through space amongst the stars.

And then beings, things, celestial bodies would agitate
against the "off-side" infraction on the field of the
universe.

The solo game and simplification of chronology
would make the encounter monotonous.

Varied movement for six days.

After breaking the record for resistence,
with energy spent on the formation of the world,
weak and worn-out, He'd go rest

on the choppy back of a mountain.

While his inter-universal "manager" began
an invigorating massage.

Phrase for analysis: *"Football is a Biblical sport."*

IV

The moon smiled, revealing to humanity the uplifting
example of an imaginary set of false teeth...

The whole earth had a certain lassitude... the primeval
postration of an acute and very feminine "fever"...

The place agreed on, the area of happiness forging this
lyricism by hidden design, is located in a magnificent
chalet, angular and beautiful like an adolescent
cocaine addict...

A young nobleman, a willowy squire sprung
from the landscape as if by sudden irrigation, looked
anxiously out a "gothic" window filled with light.

In his eyes a growing love could be seen for:

A feeble and very pretty little lass, with
a long nightgown and a little moon...

(Poetic, consummately poetic.)

Like a raw brushstroke, the nobleman sent
a seamless kiss tangled in his fingertips, which the
lover took care to receive in the tempting
fragrance of her mouth...

And to think that this love made a poem
ended with a neurotic husband, a wife in the curve
of tired maternity, an electric heater and a cat!

V

A silken and perfumed sheet, victim of the gluttony
of the mailbox, can often enclose behind its wax seal
a world of suggestions...

In each there are shudders of restless pulses
put in rhythmic "typing", symbolic letters...

When one thinks of how man crafts
an epistolary plot with pen and ink, one remembers
the silkworm starting the marvel of its work.

And the sight of three, four, five letters virtuously sealed
suddenly unfold a fan of speculation...

To open them, when they aren't yours, would be
an indescribable, "manifold" pleasure, blessed, rare.

In this one, who knows, might be the redness
of mincemeat... in that: the chromatic scale of jealousy...
in others: tragic challenges... gunshots fired...
suicides in embryonic state... etc... etc...

No limit: The letter is a traveling thought
in an envelope, enclosing a world of suggestions...

VI

I have here the results of a shameless and barefaced inquiry:

Strong wills work even in the shadows of the afterlife.

Great enthusiasms go beyond
the phenomenon of death.

Supernatural!

Those golfers, those very skilled golfers, with
an "entrenched" passion for the game, persist
in their favorite sport even after their death...

After a prudent time has passed (when the paltry
fiber of the flesh disappears for the cleansing
of the skeleton) they organize the symmetric space
of the cemetery into a great nocturnal tournament...

It's a real sight, alongside the clipped cypresses.
The golfers — skeletons!

Admirable, their contagion of spirit. The others
all ran to the training area to learn the game!

Even if one is upset by the sacking
of children's crypts to supply the skulls
used for balls and tibias for clubs...

The spectacle, though macabre,
is essentially athletic!

VII

The street took on a strange air of importance,
the moment the lady with the monocle appeared
wrapped in a gentle wind of aristocracy and panache.

We might say it was a transcendent monocle,
senatorial, dithyrambic.

With a well "stylized" gesture, she stuck the glassy
magnified eye to her own, seeming to valorize everything
that projected, what projected most from people...
shop windows... automobiles...

There was a sensation of danger, of scrutiny,
in people who knew they were being focused on,
"stripped" by the spying ability of the lady's monocle,
and moved away — after being seen — as if they carried
an approval from the audit office on their back.

But... what astonishing disillusion! When the impertinent
lens fell, hanging, back onto the velvet hatband,
the lady assumed a modest demeanor, vulnerable,
ridiculous, just like a molted bird.

VIII

I knew a person with great
gastronomic anxieties!

He had a 25HP stomach, a phenomenal stomach
with the voracity of a gigantic octopus!

And his head thought, his character oriented him, his
body
worked under the influence of that waxy transforming sac!

Five liters of chyme and five kilos!

A ravenous super-human!

When he looked at the moon you felt like comparing him
to a fat oyster in a state of pregnancy, ready to be served.
To him the stars were sautés with sausage. The sun
Was an immense egg with a double yolk poached
in the frying pan of the sky!

Once he looked at a naked woman and longed for her,
not as a woman, but as a stew *a la florentina*.

Grand idea!

The woman fried, seasoned, crisped, ready
to be eaten with salad and potato wedges!

The woman cooked with the appearance
of a stretched out chicken with mutilated feet!

Wearing for greater appeal a little 20 centimeter
piglet in her mouth, two heads of lettuce over her
kid gloves and a necklace of baby radishes
and carrots on her breast!

IX

A fiancé ready to pair the happiness or misfortune
of his life with that of another, has the idea
of a terrible Examiner of Accounts...

Accredited in his role, from the start
he "chips away" mercilessly at the life,
habits, conduct of his betrothed.

(And the revision of so much accumulated value is
terrible.)

He justifies or dismisses her conduct,
with a premature... awesome... solemn authority.

He revives the "little inquisitor devil" beneath
his everyday looks and reigns over the pre-nuptial period
like a demanding and despotic minor tyrant.
He controls precisely... progressively... with a smile...
a greeting... the unfolding of a phrase...

(There is a moment of humor. The one writing these
lines smiles violently — harshly — gently.)

*Will the Examiner of Accounts at the Solemn Moment find
the Final Balance closed?*

X

How pleasant and suggestive a couple in love is!

It doesn't matter if both are: beautiful or ugly, white or black.

It doesn't matter if they're saturated with airy Platonism
or earthy human passion.

They are in love! They have first-rate charm: poker hearts
playing for life in a love connection at its limit.

Eva in short skirt and Adam in gray trousers
in the 20th century, before they taste
the sour fate of the camuesa apple.

They pass and attract admiration. As a couple
they feel invincible.

The poorest, skinniest creatures, humble
and "scrawny", look delicious when accompanied
as they stands up straight with pride, self-worth,
full confidence.

Beautiful couple in love! — Arrogant,
as their vital reserve still hasn't divided
in the fullness of a child.

Happy because the world of paradise is theirs.

Insolent, — diabolic, — murderous, because
they don't care if they kill the innocence of angels.

Man and woman have something of gods, of gods that judge the solitary with indifference and compassion from their sky of giants.

XI

In my cabinet of outlandish ideas, there is
one that is semi-scientific: the weight of words.

When science has taken the pulse of the world
demonstrating the "indemostrable", when we have
the rapidity of thought in algebraic formulas
and the fusion of cerebral neurons in chemical ones,
other formulas in a period of perfection will offer us a

LAW OF WEIGHT FOR CLAUSES

How tiny, how subtle the little weights will be!

What a challenge of synthesis will aerate the atmosphere!

Contrary to what occurs at the moment, the work
that weighs least will acquire most value and be identified
with "New World" creation.

I support the discovery.

Atrocious cases of death have been recorded — due to
the size and weight of items.

Long clauses weighed down with lead sink us
To the bottom, while the straightforward dialectic
of short phrases keeps us afloat. They serve us
like cork toys against sinking.

Only in politics is the abundance of hot air

justifiable. The style of the great politician is to go deep
into the crowd, overwhelm reason with excess
and seize control when his audience is half dead.

Once the weight of words is established,
the Happy Reign shall commence.

XII

If spouses were strategic, the occasions
for divorce would decrease...

Without dangerous requests, homes would be
true "radii" of happiness...

Man is pleasant when (1)... beguiled (2)... submissive
(3)... inoffensive (4)... affordable (5)... trappable (6)...
in the hours of the morning, when his world
consists of a cup of coffee and the columns
of the daily paper.

One could say he disperses... "depersonalizes"...
is subverted...

Beside the array of world events, differences
at home assume microscopic insignificance.

What significance can the request for a silver fox fur
costing a thousand pesos have, when the state of Vedoble
must pay 50 millions in reparations to X?

What does the neglect of the skilled cook mean,
when thousands are dying of starvation,
unemployed workers of Y?

What is the flirting of a wife compared to the levities
and scandals of Countess Z?

Now you see...

Everything will seem trivial and small to a husband, compared to the great calamities his favorite newspaper relates; and neutralized by the pleasant smell of roasted coffee...

XIII

Pirula doesn't eat. Pirula doesn't love her sawdust doll.
Pirula is "unmoored" in the uncertain passage
from childhood to girlhood.

One could say on the threshold of a second life...

The past was a little monkey, a bear, some
cardboard children...

The future she envisions as a blond gallant,
an apple picker "ready to be picked" and complicit,
a moon with a bite from it giving light...

We won't say which existence smiles more.

A premature and false maternity napping
in a 2 cm cradle or a mustache elegantly trimmed
in preparation for hours of love...

But... let's complete the "situation" of the first section:
Pirula doesn't eat. Pirula doesn't love her sawdust doll.
Pirula is "unmoored".

She has a great worry in her blonde little head (logical
location).

Is the bitterness of life stirring?

Will she shed light on a philosophical precept?

No...

She is simply wondering if Adam and Eve,
in accordance with social formulas,
exchanged rings or not before the nuptial bleeding...

XIV

One can't deny the efficacy of graphology. Three
ellipses, a phrase in italics, two loving
parentheses that hook onto a phrase by both
"little sides" have an eloquence that's absolute...
unique... unyielding...

All symbols play the role of great instigators
on the loose, provoking readers toward a second
hidden intention by coordination or subordination
of thought...

Quotation marks — they're the Solomonic
and fairminded judge who gives to Caesar
what is Caesar's, recognizing the true authors
in the abundance of little phrases transcribed ("").

Ellipses are malicious friends, scoundrels,
dilettantes, that cleverly insinuate
a vicious, refined and subtle meaning (...).

The parentheses suggest an associated concept, a
closed, virtuous phrase — demonstrating
some idea separated from the majority.

Words in italics. Ah! Words in italics with their bent
torso, their concept so deep and remarkable...

XV

What symmetry, what "regulated" accuracy exists
in a tin of sardines!

Looking at it gives the idea of a bed in a hotel where
ten unexpected guests are looking for accommodation
to spend the night...

So it seems that the likeable sardines, with a very broad
sense of *human* solidarity (the preceding word
is a force of habit) united on their own
to cross the ocean and occupy the shop of provisions
as an example of union that doesn't let any gap
of relief appear, even for a small movement...

Their motto: "Feet by heads" serves as an accommodating
lesson for many circumstances of life...

A statesman... a fickle politician... an opportunistic
little employee... a fair-weather revolutionary... achieve
a great deal accommodating their heads to the feet of their
superior at the moment...

And so that they may affirm this without fail:
let a jet of tomato sauce or olive oil, fall on them
to conserve them in position, just like
the delicious and "symmetric" sardines...

XVI

What unexpected phenomenon, what complex
Transformation did Juanin, the smiling man, suffer?

Perplexity... (A perplexity in essence and tenfold sense.)

Great perplexity...

Juanin, who met life with an enormous smile,
contagious, tropical like a sirocco...

Juanin, who did not know algebra... the chemical
formula for cerebral neurons... the precise
velocity of thought... but who possessed
the elastic happiness of a smiling mouth.

Juanin, who checked his emotions within
distance of the square at the tip of his nose.

SUDDENLY HE FELT SAD.

His heart burning with anguish got "hung up"
whispering: Neurasthenia. Pain. Weight of
Responsibility. Conscience.

What happened?

Just that Juanin (dining at a cheap restaurant)
through a slip-up by the chef, along with
his fried steak, swallowed a piece
of the TRAGIC SENSE OF LIFE.

XVII

A wit said the methodical women who
"timetable" their loves with a tyrannical watch
are like the bottles at the pharmacy dispensed by
medical prescription, with the compulsory instruction
of one dose per hour, on the label stuck to the cylinder
that pleads: SHAKE BEFORE USING.

The scene is sly and disconcerting.

It has the makings of a super-event.

The comparison with the methodical life the clock
demands:
comprehensible and acceptable.

But that line "shake before using" has the luster
of a metaphorical composite with quintuple meaning.

If a fragile creature were atrociously shaken with
both hands as if she were an ordinary flask, to the extreme
that the compound contained became froth
— What would become of her?

She would resemble a victim of strong epilepsy, in such
a pitiful state she wouldn't look appealing in the slighest.

Now tell me if the scene evoked by the phrase
isn't suggestive —.

XVIII

The lottery!

How the crowd awaits in an exalted and selfish
mood for the arrival of the number awarded with the jackpot!

Admirable, the hope sustained in those days
by vessels of all shapes and sizes.

The rich to be richer, the poor to ascend to rich.

All are cannibals swallowing raw impatience
in their putting on and taking off of hopes.
Suffering souls with gleaming eyes who are damned,
damned awaiting the jackpot.

Here's a piece of reasoning:

To buy a ticket with the same number
of probabilities as tickets sold is stupid.

More advantages bloom from the lottery of matrimony.

One acquires the ticket for the price of champagne
the day of the wedding, sticks one's hands in one's pockets
and in the unfailing way that governs the average
human specimen, when the ninth month is out,
one is presented in living printed letters: THE PRIZE!

And what a prize! With the squeals of a piglet, with joy
and... with a bill from the gynecologist...

XIX

The safety seal is the hermetic fastener of all deposits
that can be opened. With it all metallic
contents take on an untouchable aspect.

In the seal there is material evidence of security,
great security.

The inventor of the seal must have suffered from severe
distrust, and once his invention was discovered
and patented, satisfied, he must have put seals
on the filter, the neck of the wine bottle, his wife's
virtue, the glass on the cupboard, etc., etc.

Beyond the ordinary seal, there are spiritual seals,
in which with great fuss one can seal life
with the stamp of optimism.

What a face the observer makes when he examines
a seal. He wants to find it intact, untouched.

Sealed things are lent certain importance
as if they were security boxes that harbor great
riches.

There they are, seals with bas-relief, with character,
with the exclusive mark of the seal trimmer,
faithfully awaiting their devirginization,
by a force with tremendous contempt!

XX

During many sleepless nights — awake and brooding —
I imagined the pessimist man.

In a game of ideas, I thought of him in multiple ways,
"bolted" to the bedposts, standing out like the shadow
of a different species from the usual shadow of the country
house...

I reeled off: "The pessimist man will have
to sport a dark tight-fitting suit" (logically: a light
and loose-fitting suit would result in a satisfied smile).

By association of ideas I went on: "He must be tall,
all alone, scrawny, with no backside" (with this
consideration, a mischief fled from my mind to my vision).

Then, by contiguity: "He'll have a surly attitude,
and be bitter as a jar of mustard."

Great was my admiration and noisy the shaking
of the foundations of my imaginative conviction,
when at last I met the pessimist man.

He was short, squat, with space and lightness
in his suit, and a creamy sweet mouth...

XXI

The ladies' necklines curve like great
question marks about what is to come.

Often one can believe metaphorically that a tempting neckline
is the hall of a great hotel due to the notes of a delicious jazz-band,
emerging as a discreet and harmonious sound
from the necklaces of fantastic stones.

The heron-like woman appears more like a heron
and is told one could make an anatomical study
of her long neck, counting the veiled bones in the skin.

The obese woman appears more obese,
and that naked concentric circle shows in clear form
the reserve of fat she contains.

The neckline is a piece of merchandise
unwrapped a bit on one side, which customers
touch carefully with the tips of their fingers
to learn its quality.

How distinguished is the mysterious woman
who wears a high collar in a crowd of vulgar necklines!

It seems to proclaim: "Imagine the smoothness
And color of my ten-thread silk.

Go on then.

Imagine it."

XXII

The sky? A bell jar of porcelain.

The day? Wearing a sackcloth of beauty,
suffering the martyrdom of a beautiful woman
in front of another beautiful woman.

The garden? A blossoming of tight buds
on the cherry and peach trees.

The woman, rose-matte, with a petal complexion,
reads a tiny page beneath the complicity
of foliage in flower.

UNGRATEFUL ONES!

And you still say, confronted with this picture,
that the world has nothing pleasant?

*

"Light... serpentine... ethereal... the pale woman
passes in the clear transparency of morning.

The whiteness of the charmeusse that covers her
kisses the whiteness of her flesh, and the light
kisses the conjunction of whitenesses.

When she walks, her step is a liturgy of dance.

Her pure lines tempt sculpture.

Her lilting voice murmurs tender words
of love in the morning.

Dance. Sculpture. Song in the woman-amphora..."

says the contemplative poet to the vulgar typist
walking to work.

Lyricism does what it can!!

XXIII

Dice shaker. Central Station of Luck.

Dice: Marble trains that arrive
with the mystery of black dots.

Trains on religious pilgrimage during holidays. Local trains at
other times. Presidential express trains that arrive in
bundles.

Elation, desperation are directed at them,
always in sight of impatient eyes.

Do you understand?

It's the glory-game of dice. A panoply of emotions
caught at the edges. A minute of luck
in man as an assembly of flesh and soul.

One night I saw a journalist play: With the same agility
with which he arranges words, he flipped over the dice shaker;
with the same vigor with which he shakes together reports
he jumbled the dice, just like a little crucible of pearls.

*Important warning: This chapter has a vertebra
on the next page.*

D I C E
           D I C E
                      D ICE

The engineering age will make the world
an enchantment of iron.

Living material will be stuffed and kept in museums,
like primitive anthropopithecus remains.

Man will end by oiling himself up and measuring
his capacity for consumption.

He will suffer from
iron deficiency fever.

He will dance to the melody of lethargic
"churrigueresque" honks from musical airplanes
that race and turn the sky dark.

But
        THE DICE
                        Always unscathed. Always company
for the man that flings its numbers
toward the four cardinal points.

Always the wings of happiness for whomever
plays dice under the supervision of a stylish woman,
with a smooth Havana in his mouth.

Renovation of the foundations. Reign of Luck.
New Year's Eve party. When the woman of this century
throws dice, she gambles for six or so nice boyfriends.

XXIV

The time is already dead when a woman
was compared metaphorically to a siren...
a star... or a flower...

In the frugality of the current time one cannot
apply the outdated adjective in style: "Seductive".

Sighs... fainting in an artistic pose...
romantic exclamations on moonlit nights...
are gone along with footwear with elastic and tongues...

The most "abracadabra" spectacle in this century of
the automobile and love in American gold... would be the
suicide
of passion... via the absurdity of posthumous letter.

Today is different... There is progress... There are
phenomena...

The woman of 1936-37 feels herself a suffragist...
chauffeur... aviator... driver... concert pianist...
boxer...

She has the very special quality of having a heart
replaced with a portable calculator...

They even say that every five years, she simplifies
her wardrobe with five items fewer, for the ease
of boarding the bus and sitting on the uncomfortable
public benches...

XXV

A woman who is beautiful in a feline way, —
through an atavistic leftover of sadism —
colors her nails with a bloody polish that
dyes red the aura where her fingers play.

It's distinguished, but it seems those present
were steeped for two minutes in intense tragedy:
the epilogue of a crime or a religious rite, in which
an innocent little lamb was sacrificed.

The red nails, violently red, like rubber
reflectors, give the shivers to all those nearby
and everyone else, and through a link of ideas,
evoke ghostly hands stirring a red
labyrinth of viscera... innards...

The edges, in contrast, look greenish or
yellowish, like... (Pardon the attempt to set up
an antihygienic metaphor.)

Many times I've considered the possibility
of mutilating the fingers of women who infringe
upon civic tranquility with the criminally
red polish of their feline nails.

XXVI

All lives have a worn-out, shabby pattern
of sensation. The faculty of "feeling" a new way
is inscribed radially in a very limited field.

Not even the existence of the beggar
whose stomach is at the mercy of passer-by
can acquire the grace of the "unexpected" or "unusual".

The only role somewhat worthy of envy
is the anarchist agitator of destructive make.

For he lives on the edge of "perhaps" and "circumstance",
at the scale of a diabolical, dissolving,
explosive, sinister Antichrist.

He knows the life that moves around him: the rail
of a train, the voyage of a ship, etc., depend
on the bomb he places, to channel
everything onto the path of death.

He truly questions "tomorrow", not knowing
if when dawn comes at the window, it will sing
the glory of leadership, liberation from the gallows,
or fifty days of hunger and prison.

What's more — he has the noblesse of not pursuing an end,
an object, personal wealth.

Here I've explained why the life of the extremist agitator
can be attractive and novel.

XXVII

When does one measure the vastness of misfortune?

When one is bored.

One must expand purgatory to accommodate tired souls!

To live with one's desire empty, unoccupied. To not know
what the spirit wants to achieve, to be a star... a worm...
glory... or failure...

To feel useless, ridiculous, silly, without an ambition
that grounds a pride in living.

To despise romanticism for its delicacy trimmed
in the heavens... To hate materialism
for its sarabande of sick flesh...

To loathe the rest as perverse... cruel... hypocritical...
unloyal... treacherous...

To loathe oneself, recognizing the same faults,
as one belongs to the same species...

To see the past as black, *idem* the future...

That...

That is boredom...

XXVIII

When one has a fever for discovering calligrammatic
likenesses, similar signs can be found among
the most opposite, logically irreconcilable bodies:

A skinny dog can seem like a svelte woman.

A gentleman the rhombus of a mosaic.

And a formless and "jellyfishlike" slug like.............
(here the reader may fill in the similarity that strikes her).

I have shown here how the comparison of a human
organism to the bodywork of a car conveniently
covered with a nickel-plated mask that
represents epidermic protection is viable.

When science seals the arc of all knowledge,
a mechanic, an expert mechanic will technically classify,
in a vivisectioned organism, the pumps, pistons,
connecting rods, valves and belts,
different organs of the human body...

May God save me from such a classification...!

XXIX

No one can praise the clever!

The most elegant link, the silkiest words,
the firmest connection of phrases and concept,
are not the merit of the author herself.

Everyone when writing, sprinkles in specifics
left over from texts read... words that make an impression
on one's consciousness... memories... endless quotations
that subconsciously call our attention
and are stratified in memory.

We could say that words are catalogued
on the cerebral shelf, put there by the infinite authors
that have presented us with their language, and that
for us there is only the labor of ordening.

Analyzed with rigor we are something like
"secondhand clothes dealers" for the rest, since we use
— as vulgar usurpers — the words, phrases, and useful
clauses we pick up reading, with a certain modality
of our own expression...

Kids who whistle, in or out of tune,
songs that aren't our own!...

XXX

To be hungry!

I have here a feeling that is subliminal,
apostolic, human and above all decent.

A face "fakirized" by hunger, by weakness,
transubstantiated into the enchanted materiality of clay,
can constitute a supreme work of art. The muscles
— in a hypertension of anxiety, of exploded will,
of craving that doesn't find a bite of sustenance,
reflect a psychological more than physiological
phenomenon.

By contrast: How repugnant, how coarse does that man seem
with a porcine double chin, who noisily gnashes his
molars, feeding himself, in preparation for what's next,
undoing, anti-assimilation.

When they tense, the fibers of our sensibility
are refined, in a flexibility of sensation:
To be hungry is a pleasure, and a great one.

To be happy, to starve! To renounce the animal nature
of eating, for the bodilessness of not eating!

When one eats, when one sates oneself,
the charm is broken. One arrives at the
disastrous state of the water carrier
who has filled his vessel with mud.

XXXI

To feel infinite, "pushy", marvelous ideas
bustle in the brain.

To be completely overflowing with thoughts
that know no channel, that with a force and intensity
of their own "multipolarize", producing themselves...

How?

One idea generates another, and another, with the
gradation
of concentric circles of water produced with a touch.

To imaginatively contemplate their harassment,
their demands for the right of written intelligibility
... imploring to be translated, instilled with life
in the symbolism of language...

(Each idea — ultimately feminine —imperiously demands
the brilliance, the precision of the word.)

One could say that ideas group together in the mind,
desiring quick coupling on paper.

And then...

The words, the concepts, the clauses, in all
their profundity, their eloquence, their meaningful world
and combinatory capacity, are lost... they don't want
to present themselves ... without knowing that

in doing so they kill us with their absence...

Martyrdom...

This torment that surpasses anything
imagined by the Inquisition... we all suffer it...
and what a shame...: it is common...

XXXII

A piece of bread following five days of fasting
must taste to the palate like a piece of glory with yeast.

A "trembling" and explosive kiss after an agony-
abstinence will be the vision of paradise
in all its splendor and lushness.

An electric stove after two hours of cold
on a barren plain revives the blood.

An unassailable principle: Continuity reduces
the wealth of sensations.

Intermittences show more selection,
more liveliness and taste.

If one contemplates the sunset every day,
it no longer satisfies our pictorial sense.
To work... to eat... to sleep without fail,
makes ennui reign in this immense
witches' coven we call world.

All these activities carried out after great
lapses of time would lose their ordinariness
and clearly unpleasant routine.

(*I believe we will find the common denominator of
innovated pleasure when we learn how to arrange
our reality by dividing it up in sensations
with great intervals of rest.*)

Only then will life be an "inexhaustible" source of finite days!

XXXIII

Why at the end of the sparkling, risqué
pictures of love reaching their last "stage"
is an imaginary Intertype keyboard
in 20 point font what follows?

Why is the scene... the final scene...
"crammed" with crude realism presented
with a bracket of ellipses like this?

"..."

The representation is suggestive.

It implies an unheard social injustice.

It summarizes a trampling on the moral conscience of the
individual.

Why are we going to give ellipses the ridiculous
and "go-between" mission of representing salacious
scenes?

Out of a principle of high equity, we must limit
their ubiquity, before they are perceived in their
role as the "jokers" of language, in the most awful
and runaway passages of love in its final stage...

PART TWO

Diagram of a metropolis located between the four cardinal points of the imagination.

Dear sweet readers: you will give me your assent
little by little with nods of the head: (with this amusing
proof you will be rendered distinguished or ridiculous:)

Irregular network of streets... central... intermediate...
"suburban"...

Fantasy hotels: double and wide-ranging musical
entertainment based on the blues and synchronized leg kicks.

Luminous warnings: points of flame that with their candlesticks
say with flickering tongue: yes... no... yes... no...

Luxurious feminine silhouettes: pendulums of modern
agitation ... (First wrapping: an elastic corset. Last: a
fur coat.)

Jostled walks down the avenues of style. (The tumults
on the current of the avenue considered an intestinal tube
are undigestible obstacles).

"Subjectivization": Collisions... collisions of jazz...
of love... of automobiles...

METROPOLIS: Americanism, copied on
an octavo of carbon paper.
Prawn stir fry. Sarabande of naked
and clothed madness.

Additional note: Think of the insubstantial content
of this reading.

ONE

"Quiet Mrs. Fox, Mr. Lion, Mr. Horse. Move forward
Mrs. Crane, Mr. Cylinder, Mr. Piston," said Basterra in
a language of atavistic new words.

He had to design capital letters and personalize
the representation of iron in these forms:
Crane-Cylinder-Piston, which are characters belonging to the Ltd
of the modern metropolis.

Stage design 1936: Network of telephone wires.
Factories, telegraph booths, merit more reverence
than pastoral fields with cows, ducks and earthworms.

The last neorhythmic style the machine sings, as a
long-feathered duster sweeps away everything sentimental,
everything corrupted by the delicacy of the old school.

Serious attempt: To cook up metaphors at low pressure
before the vulgar moon tattoos nocturnal cats
with its web of light.

What's more — have you thought that the noise of the motors
and power plants make the cemeteries less gloomy?

Even death itself — let's suppose a high current
carbonization — no longer comes from flashy formulas...

A wink... and at a speed of 300 kilometers per
hour a soul flies to the sky astride the steam
of the electric machine.

TWO

How beautiful life is in a semidelirium
of cocktail and jazz!

Colored race: twin sons produced in North America.

Cocktails: Fifth distillation of the grape.
Drops of lemon (flora).

Jazz: Dark man who blows in the saxophone (fauna).

Saxophone: Incomparable sweet-talking instrument
into which one breathes notes (gea).

Triangle. Shamrock essence of nature
in the closing moments of the 20th century.

Thigh-high stockings. Fine pelt — for women.

Walk-over shoes. Shiny seal rings — for men.

With cocktails and jazz one loses
chronological track of time.

When one hears the saxophone the restlessness
of the rhythm is epileptic. One wants to pour out
the last drop of illusion — An aperitif to dance steps,
to mark the final harmonic rat-a-tat.

The choppy transition of plates makes channels
in the movements and the dancers' feet weave figures

that make new holes in the floor.

While the cocktail dances a slow and streaky blue
with the malic acid of the restaurant dessert,

here's a phrase for analysis: *Satan is beautiful because he dances
to infernal jazz and loads up with fiery cocktails.*

THREE

To feel the life of the city with full intensity,
One must flee from logical limits and the pre-established,
Rejuvenating sensibility with new "tape reels".

Consider that a high percentage of suicides
originate in boredom, that one must avoid
conveniently "anti-septisizing"
... the spirit.

When ennui threatens, to the point I could
inhabit very strange roles,

I imagine myself as:

Official inspector of pedestrians.

Delicate artist of the football fields.

Dedicated controller of canine flirts.

Overseer of waste.

Representative of the sewers.

And when I write the next line, fatigue has fled,
revolutionized, overcome by fright
like an acolyte deserted by love...

FOUR

In a show of its gray inner lining, taking off its hat,
the city says "Good afternoon".

Greeting from 6 to 6.30 pm.

A half hour that languidly charms its way
through the passage of day and night.

The electric globes ponder whether they should
light their insides.

Decimal fraction of time in which the feeble joker
hidden by domestic habits is attracted by the
street, the automobile, love, fried food.

We are men of the twilight, not in the sense
of "The Night of the Ages", but through
the unhealthy drive that the afternoon dissolving
in shadow operates on us.

6 pm and the street is a captivating tease.

One can admire the softening of the sky, the under-eye circles of
a solitary tigress or the carts that have something of the desert
in their dromedary hump.

(A voice says these "autos" find themselves pregnant.
Through a physiological aberration, they give the world
motorbikes, like palpable memories of love
with rented bicycles.)

And over the course of this half-circumference of the clock,
snob chimneys sigh with passion, and kisses at a distance
are sent from telephone poles to electric pylons.

All is a palpitation of life and love
in the civic canyons.

Hour of greeting: 6 to 6.30 pm.

FIVE

At three in the afternoon, the roads appear
half-bored.

People who walk in the midday sun
look like little terracotta figures, surprising
in the artifice, the immobility of their different poses,
some artistic and others not at all.

Whoever goes to the mailbox to throw in some letters...
whoever goes to the grocery store to buy matches...
whoever goes to the office heavy with
shadow has an air of fatigue...

It seems they carry the prologue of the night,
when they will sleep, and find voluptuousness
in closing their eyes.

All the walkers carry the obsession of the CHAISE
LONGUE, and it seems they think:

"If at the next turn, if under that little tree,
if behind this trellis, there were only a chaise longue
for a siesta"

as these comfortable furniture items for idleness
rest in half-shadow, behind closed doors, not knowing
how they obsess the tired at three in the afternoon.

SIX

Elegant husbands, in the theater, in the pastry shop,
in the stadium, leading their atavistic and
beautiful wives by the arm, have something of the clumsy
salesman about them, in the annoying task of exhibition...

He squeezes them in a remote approximation
to the man who displays his items...

Generally they have a measured step, like a caravan
of notoriety, or a Squadron Sergeant
bandying himself about in a patriotic parade.

And the women, guided in this form of protection
before the public, sensing the pride of possession, feel
like protected dolls, feeble, beautiful, big girls...

Very amusing.

When there's already a handful of kids on the way,
they transfer fifty percent of their quality as
exhibitionists to the LADIES.

Then:

Husband and wife, with a self-satisfied and placid air,
transform into proud salesmen of their
little puppets...

SEVEN

The automobiles pass with a music of satisfied motors, muffled...

They glide slowly caressing the asphalt...

In beauty and artistry they are like bottles of cologne...

They are defined musically by their melodic lines,
their micro-saxophonic horns...

(What verse will be discovered with the rhythm found
in the movement of the "auto"?)

This smooth, glass-windowed car is the reflection of the aristocratic
idler who loses faith and strength of will.

Why does man subordinate his legs of undeniable
vitality to tires at the mercy of the pressure gauge?

In the automobile, excess is born. Those who move
in it, accustomed to the collapse of landscapes,
long still more for the collapse of humanity.

Those men enthused by wheels, crowbars,
bodywork don't feel the fine down of things...

Even cars with soft seats to offer
quash activity, the energy of generations.

Look at the car I mentioned at the start, conveying a lazy
millionaire, and ridiculous childish enough to pass me...

EIGHT

Buses are a category of slave.

The Social Revolution will have to inform them
of the advantages in favor of their liberation.

While aerodynamics can run their elegance
throughout the urban radius, following the stretch of the
imaginary arrow, slave buses, shackled to a tired route,
are limited to coming and going down a single avenue.

With a small fourth conversion, let's look
at the air of complicity of those who occupy
the seats of a bus.

For the first time in his life the man with his handlebar
mustache brushes with his stylized trouser leg the girl
in white ankle socks. The lady with the smoky eyeglasses
sits happily alongside the kid with gray trousers.

In that human crush moving at high speed,
it seems time contagiously runs
in a hurry, and there is a clear complicity
of adventure for 5 minutes.

When the driver sees that in one afternoon, someone
has taken the same bus four times with a worried look,
there is suspicion. The notion comes to him
that the person is a counterfeiter of money
or a breathtaking executioner of tender lives.

NINE

A little secret of the profession:

The able drivers of automobiles that "cram"
the streets of the city, and break in their wild horns,
destroying their nervous system, must have one
obsession: the Traffic Arrow.

In the dubious shadow of the afternoon,
on the dark paths of night, they will follow it,
along with the "dustdevils" of speed.

The same skill must influence the mentality
of the Guide, who designs the fatal arrow
with indelible characters.

Even on the path of love, they will pursue
the womanly silhouette most similar to an arrow.

TEN

The accident darkened the city.

Even the sky found itself plated with big black
tears: A bourgeois and high-yielding airplane had
crashed into a socialist bus, "horizontalizing" it
on the asphalt.

The instinct of conservation at its greatest strength!

The rest of the buses on the convuluted roads of the city
traveled carefully and slowly with the dread of vehicles
that wait, resigned, for the plan of being
crushed.

In the blue mosaic of morning or the dull opacity
of afternoon, they look shy, stunned,
discouraged.

The one mentioned was being repaired in the next
garage, like a man condemned to death without reprieve
who serves as an example for other delinquents,
making them participants in his great tragedy.

Poor little buses, with the lesson of the collision
fresh, they move very slowly, at the risk of repeating it
in one fateful little second...!

ELEVEN

Sometimes the aesthetic sense of the individual is naturalized
in a naked simplicity.

One wishes for simplicity in its greatest stylistic expression,
to throw out ambiguous, superfluous, vulgar ornaments,
favoring a dose of the thinning, destructive element.

I have already explained my idea
that all parks in the city should be
converted into plain sports fields.

All of them with their infinite little gardens, paths,
pools, limited four-cornered form, seem
to me refuges, great affronts to space,
to the implicit freedom of the earth itself.

The benches — headaches set there without
scruples. The trees — unbearable obstacles.

It seems to me logical to clear away the whole line
of "arboreal" and forest hindrances, to convert all
parks into airy sports stadiums.

What a shame not all think the same way!

TWELVE

Sunset in the city is different from sunset in the country.

In metaphors: The first adopts the aspect of an absolutely
free man not interfered with by influences...

The second, fatally, has the humiliation of a prisoner...

In the complicated artifice of constructions, in
the irregular mesh of avenues, which cross
like threads of a great spiderweb, twilight is
taken captive and closed in a limit-environment.
It becomes poorer. It becomes ridiculous.

Perhaps you haven't seen the devastated and small
"imprisoned" twilight that shadows the city?

But what an infinite idea comes together
in a country sunset!

Enormous, stretched-out, flattened world
on the expansive plain. Rocky mountain ornaments.
Unlimited expanse of impartial landscape, where
shadow-servants in "hiding" from the sun bow down
free, proud, imposing.

THIRTEEN

We must give new attention
to the importance of public flagstones.

We must give them their place in a brochure, as they make up
the city and give perspective to the great avenues.

The flagstone was born at the rocky heart of a stone
landscape. It was strangely tired, like all
rocks born at some time lost in the origins.

Then the hand of a stonecutter chiseled it out;
geometric, cleaned of lumps and multiple edges, it
was laid into an arbitrary street.

Look at it: there, on the last urban blueprint, flat, simple,
its torso bearing all steps taken by us
— poor mammals inferior to the penguins
of France —.

Private etymological wits slander it,
reminding us the term FLAGSTONE can double
as both object and insult.*

An insult whose tessellating meanings can easily be laid down:
Dense understanding, spectacular idiocy.

Poor flagstone!

Translator's note: "Adoquín" can mean both "flagstone" and "fool", hence
Mundy's comment about it doubling as "object and insult". The "penguins of
France" likely refer to the book *Penguin Island*, by Anatole France (1908).

FOURTEEN

One day it dawned cloudy, cold, snowy, with a percentage
of raw winter.

Those living here found the morning exotic
when they admired its "wintery" appearance, as autumn
was just starting to fade.

In the full succession of burning dawns, this day
was a day embedded, out of place, like
a little false stone in the setting of a dozen
real diamonds.

A hoax by the Creator, who prepares jokes
of fickle timing to give the feeling he can trick us
whenever he feels like it.

An abrupt cold morning, under the weather
among its companions, the burning approachable
mornings that are like girls just kissed.

How many at dawn said: Starting today
it is winter! When the calendar gave them the lie
in the clear form of red numbers.

A cold and lonely sky, when the skies of the other
days were blue, marvelously blue.

All a heavenly joke...

FIFTEEN

The trees of the avenues are pale, nostalgic,
exhausted by memory.

Lined up — they constitute monochrome and stoic
individualities.

Skinny from an endemic, they're like wild circus
animals, agonizing behind bars
for lost freedom.

Fed up with urbanism, tired of the city, sick
of exhibition, they think of the secular... immense...
virgin forest of their predecessors.

They beat against their fate, loathing the daily
movement...
the artifical and decorative path... the pitiful gardens...
the fields seasoned like culinary preparations...

Not even the breath of compost invigorates them.

"Transplanted" from their great wild origin to the
ridiculous
urban shelter, they breathe with mythological, proud,
magnificent natures.

All trees suffer from seeing themselves ridiculous,
enslaved in great promiscuity in the city.

SIXTEEN

The hulking-post has blossomed into an electric lightbulb
through the miracle of the Empress of Light...

Raised over the flat vulgarity of the city,
the proud one drunkenly contemplates the "twisted"
chessboard of streets with unusual attention...

The whole neighborhood is magnetized to her vision...

She is tainted beyond hope with scandal,
indecency, street obscenity.

She knows what the back storage sheds
of houses in the neighborhood hide... the last nooks
and crannies of buildings... the inner gardens... the airy
charm of the rooftops...

In the everyday laziness, she glimpses how unclothed
and light the women look during their morning stretches,
when on the patios the first popular songs
are heard...

She satisfies her female curiosity with a far-ranging
and intimate look into all the trifles of life
of the neighborhood.

Meanwhile her stem, the faithful wood-post,
continues sustaining her like a resigned lover,
with its big-bodied and ungainly endurance...

SEVENTEEN

The frame of the atmosphere darkens...

The light bulbs come into relief...

The crowd gracefully "skirts" all the walkways.

My "ghost-swimming" spirit-diver immerses itself in the
deliquescence of night.

The city produces its weary.

One could say it crushes them in the plazas and streets
with the cigarette end of fatigue.

There are men intimidated by the clear sunlight
of day as if they were birds of night,
who grow content with the passage to shadow.

"Sketched" men of four lines
ready to be passed onto film: animated cartoons.

Men suitable for suggestive daily accounts
and novelettish stories with oblique and abnormal plots.

Men of "standard" size who charge
current life with being a hundred centimeters.

All, all living the long and anonymous hours
that precede the dawn with apathy,
with the complicity of bootleggers, counterfeiters
or petty thieves in a bar...

EIGHTEEN

Inspiration sings its flat note in the suburb.

One must contemplate it, absorb it, fill one's lungs
with its air to answer the question of its semi-urban
and semi-country soul.

In the first phase: a dissolving of "metropolis" in its
birth of the pampa. A devastating conquest
of civilization.

In the second: A field rebellion in its territory.
A primitive stagnation.

Dual perspective.

Wide streets, not devirginized by the aggressiveness
of the sewer system, naked of pavement, free of
symmetry.

Low, rustic, sparse houses. Earth tint. Pastures and
carts.

The suburb is the conyugal link between city and country.
A binomic alloy of landscapes melding the
natural and the constructed.

NINETEEN

When walking down the middle of the street
one feels a singularly exquisite pleasure...

One acquires the upstanding appearance of a Sergeant
in a parade of electric lights aligned 4 meters from
the asphalt.

And one adds to the motorized crowd with a certain vain
maneuver of defying all vehicles with slowness,

marking the rhythm in time,
and watching the trees bowed over
in an "eighteenth century" greeting.

And when one sees an automobile one says: "As long as
it's not a real donkey driving, it won't run me over."

And so it is that the cars don't crush one as they'd like
and instead pass alongside, smoothly — without doing
real harm.

But reading a police report, one realizes
there are many drivers who do not have visible
signs of being asses, yet have run over and killed people.

This risk increases the charm of walking
in the radius of the huge gliding vehicles.

75% of happiness and heroism come from not eluding
a danger in life...

TWENTY

Afternoon becomes tubercular with a gust of infectious
wind that blows from the south.

Muddy yellow earth — it makes one think of a stagnant
afternoon that lacks the rays of sun marking
the advance of the hour in the shade, the rays
that mark the passage of time.

Whistles are heard that dream of piercing
the unwilling earth, and sound like the complaints
of a patient calling desperately to the doctor.

The pulse weakens in the slow beat of a few drops
of rain.

There's no doubt about it.

In the languid afternoons, the pale and fainting one
is something like a blue-faced woman.

And one waits for tubercular day, full of
cold and despair, to rest in the pious
tomb of night!

TWENTY-ONE

I adore them: the trams — big toys. They are
calm and tranquil. If they had been seditious
anarchists, they would have ended up like those
shining "tortoiselike" cable cars, filling the streets
with insides of steel. But they are calm and tranquil...

I adore them: ornamental trams hanging from electric
wires with an expression of something being dragged along.
Their absence completely disfigures the metropolis.
It makes it ugly, like some corrosive acid's been thrown on it.

I have a very marked preference for the "tramway"
platform. I find the sense of freedom summed up there.
It seems my heavy supplications are granted when I find myself
there, next to the ladies, some of whom, if I had "binocular vision",
I'd see impertinently staring at me, as if to say: "here goes
the spiritual androgyne". — I focus my gaze. I'm not mistaken.
Some visuals are assaults of hard burning aggression.

On the platform at the last minute with all those
about to board, I have two worlds available: that of the tram
travelers childishly seated face-to-face, and that of the fleeing
artistic panorama of the city. Exercises of instant
psychology and skills of a festival photographer
focus the perspectives of the streets.

Science and art for the modest sum of twenty centavos!

TWENTY-TWO

Telephone: prison of voices. Pulp of the mechanical life.
Symbology of civilization by wire.

Telephone: Womb box of our refined gutturalisms
enclosed in a pocket dictionary.

The "standardized" zeal of our men urban
to the marrow is dictated by the command of the
telephone's loud ring, like a call announcing
a slice of daily fate.

Chirrrrrr...................... Chirrrrrr........................

A chat with numbers? A disreputable meeting, and because
it is disreputable, exquisite? Hour for a "cocktail" with
blue flavor and Africa in its shaking?

Who knows... Only when the grating ring, — appendix
of the telephone — is silenced will the mystery be torn open.

I believe the conservation of the species is maintained
because of this small latent transmitting device, which
has courteously made love punctual. And if
the dawn of Humanity was sad, it was for lack of an
automatic telephone that eased the understanding of the
"eve-adam" couple.

Sensitive...

The First Woman — who had the supremacy of Uniqueness and Sin — walked five miles to invite the First Man for an aperitif.

Nearly unemotional...

Today... today the women of the globe "infantilize themselves" before the telephone.

Rather: They prepare for the day and paradisiacal well-being of the day in front of the earphones of the whole globe.

TWENTY-THREE

Edda: Potter's clay made in the miracle of light "conjoined"
with love. A conjunction that is beauty and eurhythmics.

Edda: Harmony-vibration-note-color.

Roland: "Archetypical" man as strong masculinity,
Male of: 25 years. Roland is a ciborium
of materiality and delight.

—Do you see them?
—Yes...!

Together in the "autumnal" splendor of the afternoon —
united —
marvelously united and caressing as a morning sun
shines on a pale mosaic.

Her face impresses itself on his mind. He
grows more mediocre loving her, loving her
as a farmer does his favorite pair of oxen...

Everything is a charm.

Everything is a "whiplash" exquisite delight of love.

Suddenly: to increase that feeling, that passionate
sentimentality, that discovery of pleasure, in the midst
of the "autumnal splendor of the afternoon", she tries to sing
the "future" in notes, or what comes to the same thing:
a snatch of soft sweet song.

THE CHARM IS BROKEN

The impressionability of the lover shatters into pieces, which echo in the emptiness of the moment.

She's sung badly... she's changed the order, the harmony, with her voice bitter like lemon juice...

Roland withdraws.

Edda is musically out of tune... Starting today — due to abandonment — today she will also be out of tune with love...

TWENTY-FOUR

History is a source of life: accumulated, dead,
past and centuries old —.
One can't capture the reality of facts
that took place in old books.

Each man in the guiding light of his existence is an
unfathomable world of passions, multiple and jumbled
feelings that arrive at the unnameable. Would it
be possible for a historian to focus that reality,
penetrating into the logical order of those great worlds?

Impossible.
Bi-impossible: (Same as 2 impossibles. Limit of the impossible.)

History is nothing more than the historian. The unity of
a soul with the past it wants to "permeate",
weakly sifting through a chronology of facts
so precise, dead, pale, bland...
And yet.

Dethroned kings, beheaded on the guillotine
—nobles knocked down from their gold and power —
—serfs sacrificed in the grind of war and revolutions
a hundred or two hundred years ago — can they add
anything to the harsh intimacy of life and fullness
we enjoy in the moment?

...

...

...

TWENTY-FIVE

To see life brightly, with the most pantheistic
and "welcoming" colors, there's nothing better than
the excessive use of ellipses. In them the amusement
and subtlety of life splendidly coexist. You don't
know the intoxication of ellipses...? It can
be classified with the marvelous. When you lavishly
sprinkle those little worlds in the typewriter and article,
your heart laughs at such a trace of picaresque and irony.

Whenever I see a pedantic set of features, preserved in
many-wrinkled complacency, I say: "This man
is poor in ellipses." "He must not know about them."
And this turns out to be true... it must be...

Extreme familiarity with the marks leads
one to the unusual discovery that there
are ellipses in the voice—. In the chat of some restless
women I've found them, treacherous and intentional,
while they talk of "worldly things", drawing out
the last word with a flicker of expressive eyes...
delightfully expressive...

Let us always, always flee from stiff and severe prose,
from seriousness, from know-it-all syndrome, by trotting away on
ellipses, which a cinematographic pan might show like this:

"..."

TEN-METER WIDE ABSURDITY

A piece of mud: unformed, absurd, undecided.
(Apparently it is impossible to define the art
of a piece of mud.) It is the raw, unmodeled deposit,
"untransmitted" to any spirit, like a hypothetical virginity.

There are three artists around it. They can press it,
inflict on it the punishment of the thumb,
to create art in perfect and absolute form.

Consuming all the possibilities of creation that
arise in man, they can forge the filigree of art,
which like so much art borders the extraterrestrial.

However:

The first takes the unformed mass and makes a ball.
He creates the sphere, believing the sphere
represents intelligence and art. The spherical form rolls
(to roll is an attribute, when there is a slope that favors the
movement of the sphere).

The second penetrates the soul, with the sinuous
form of woman. It wants to model the poem of the flesh
in mud and fertilize it in beauty, stylizing perfect curves.

The third, fantastic, — fantastic, — fantastic,
live model of the Genius in this Century, raises his hand
in the zeal of condemnation, the zeal of destructive fever,
and destroys the "spherical" perfection and revitalized
woman—.

He destroys, imposing himself through destructive fever, through the fever of chaos, which is a blaze.

And the third, in the night, in the midst of darkness
— everything, in the midst of everything —, shakes
the mud in his hands, and makes exist the inexistence
of an ideal and perfect passage. Beautiful hot ash of art, illuminated
in the shock of its inner richness with the discovery of the
world...

And when in Art there are three... and two... they want
to be Gods... while the third being a Genius, is silent... for
to be silent is to make thought flower on the route to
Perfection... —.

THE
QUIXOTISM
OF
WRITING
A
BOOK
IS
CONSUMED

HILDA